This no[illegible] belongs to:

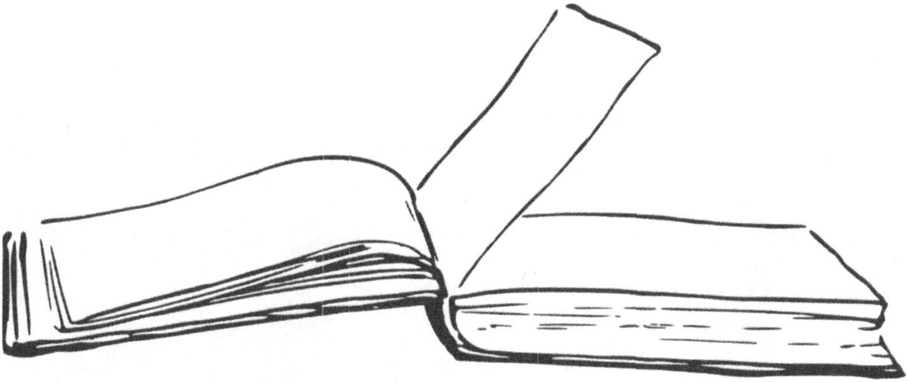

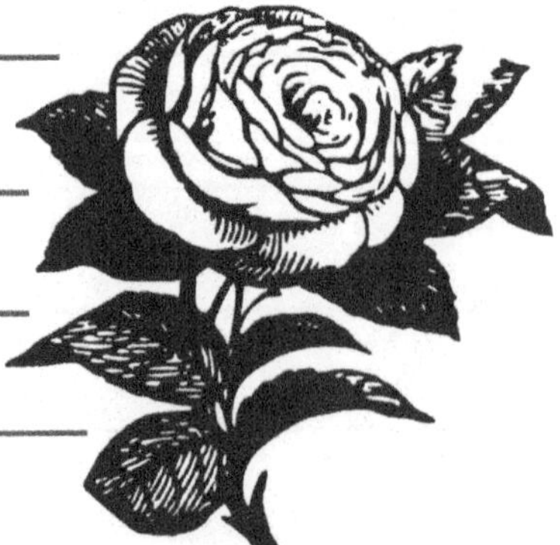

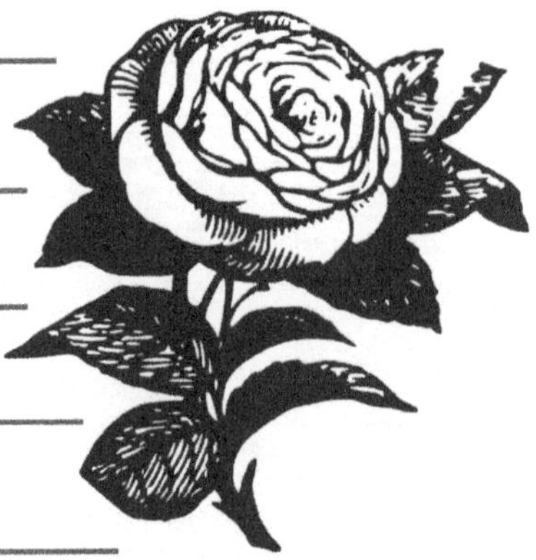

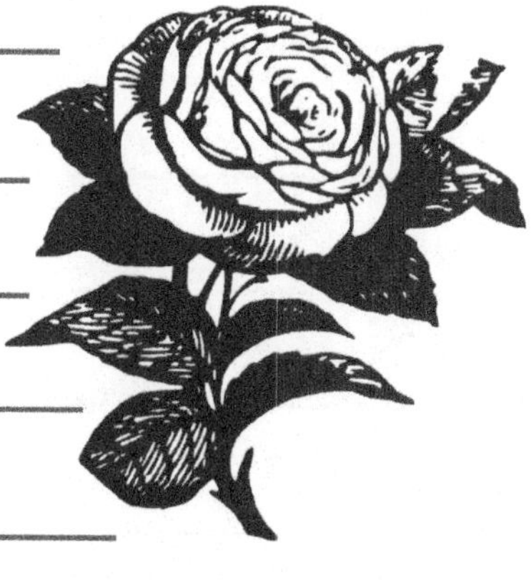

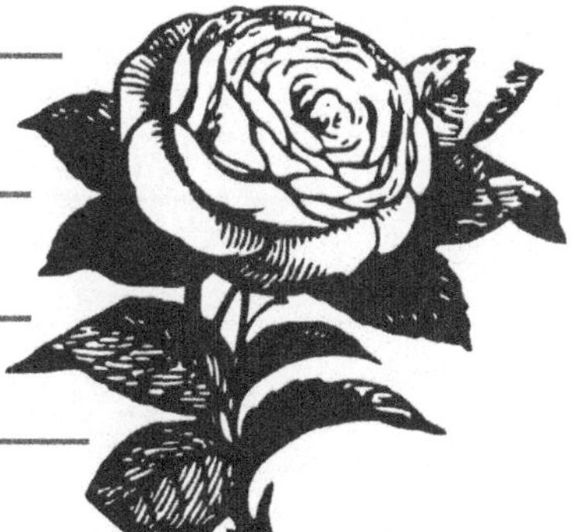

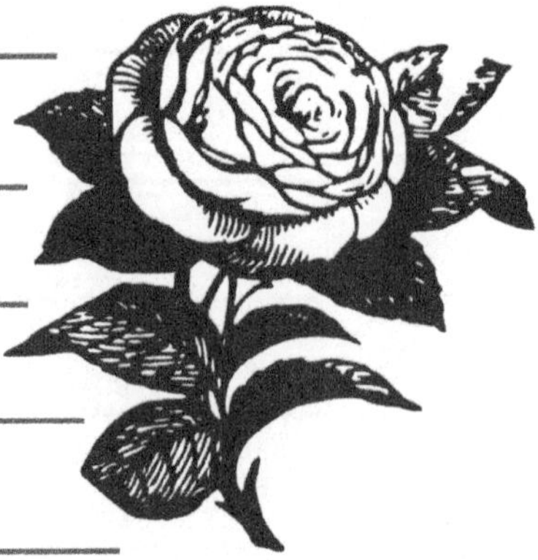

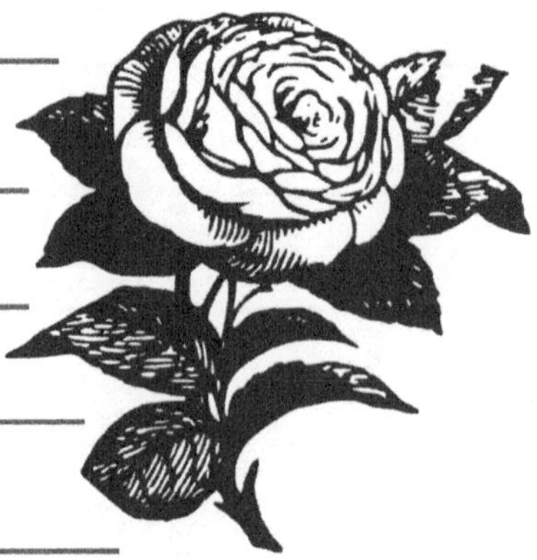

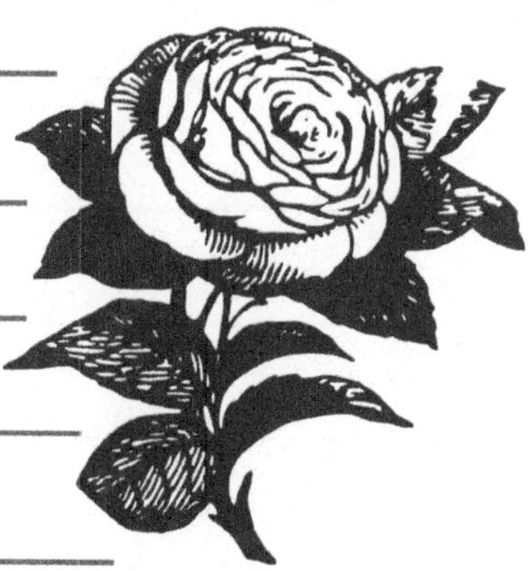

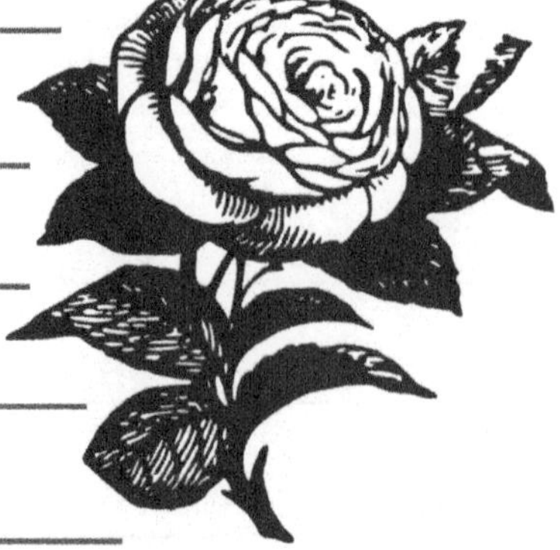

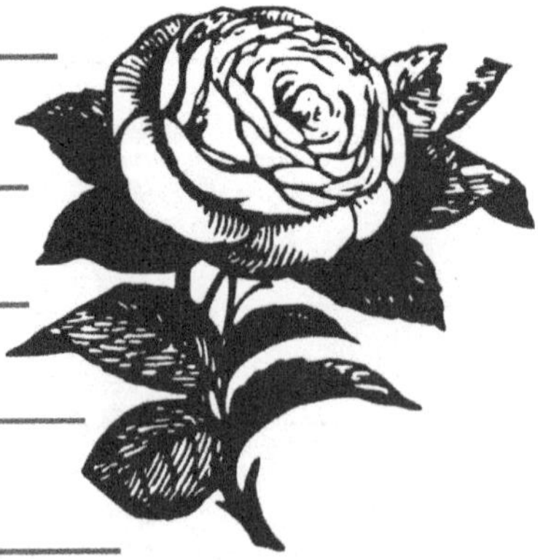

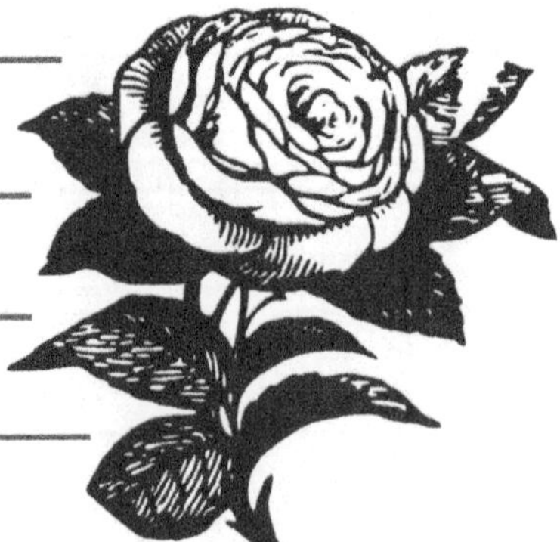

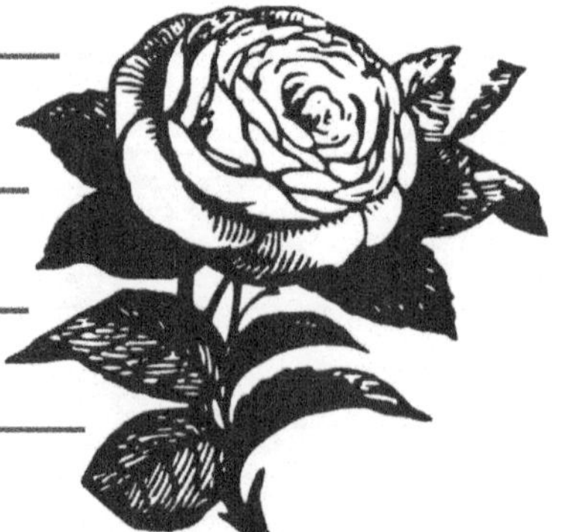

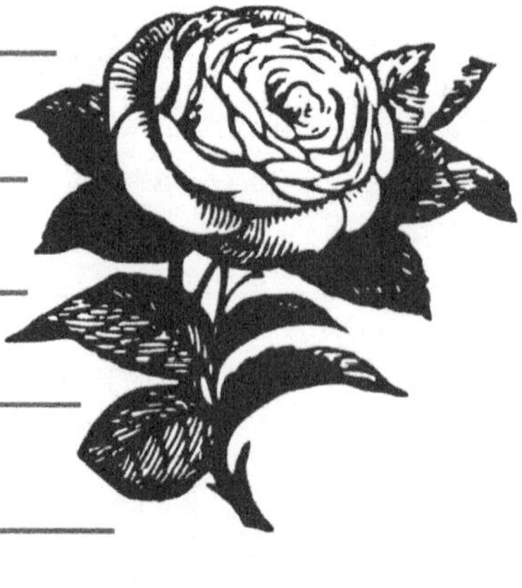

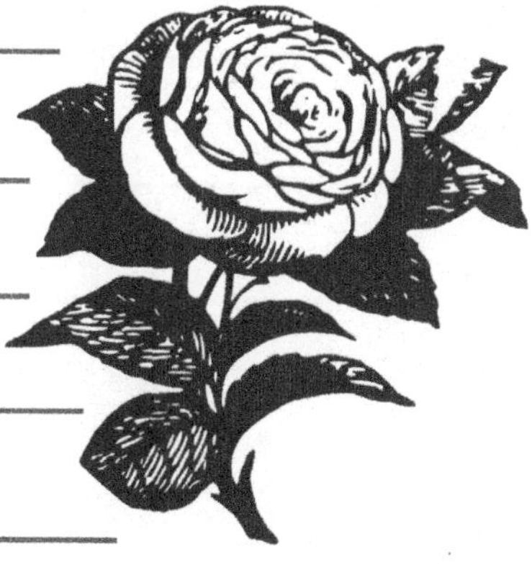

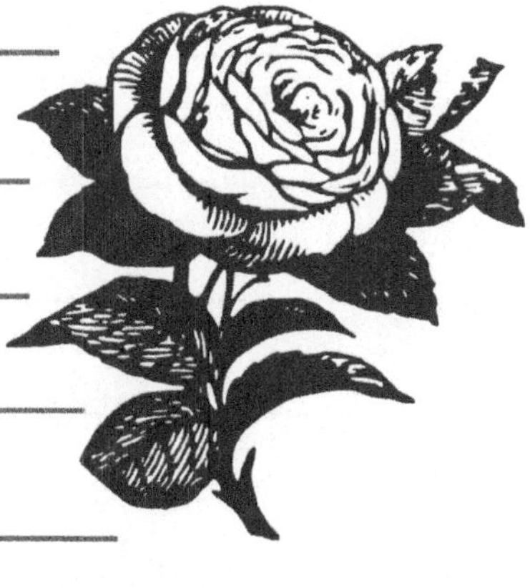

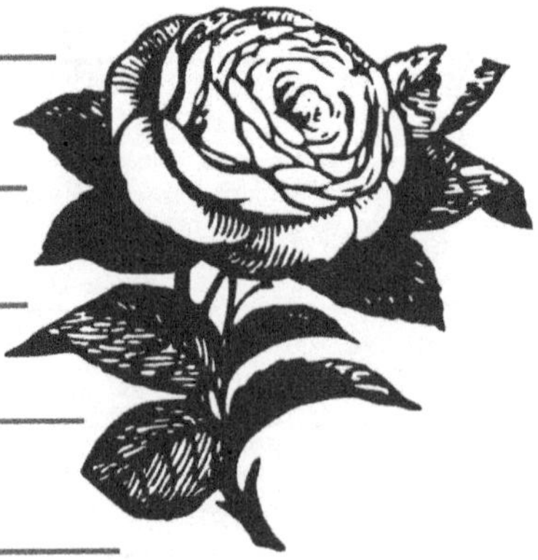

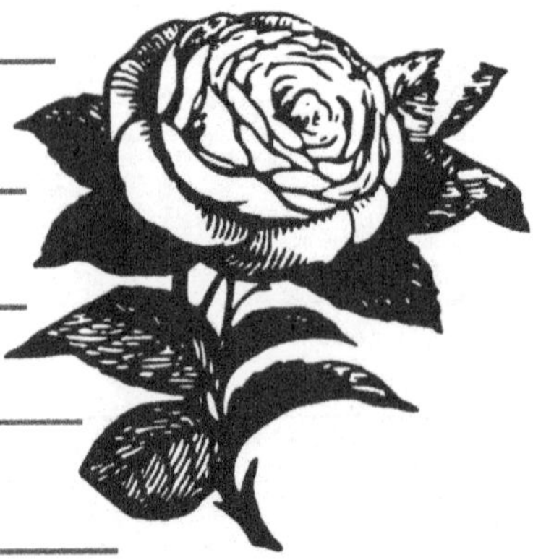

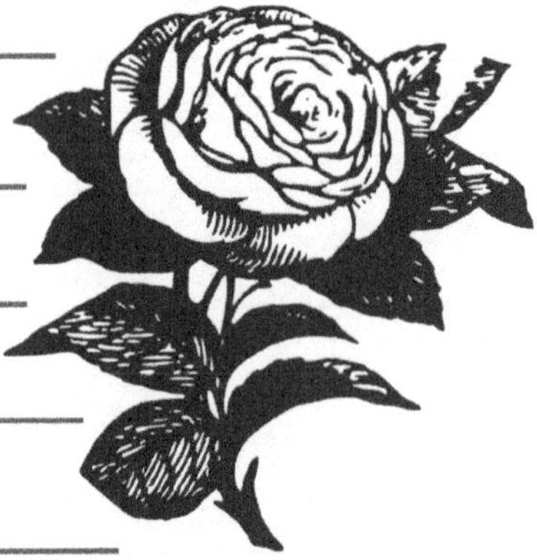

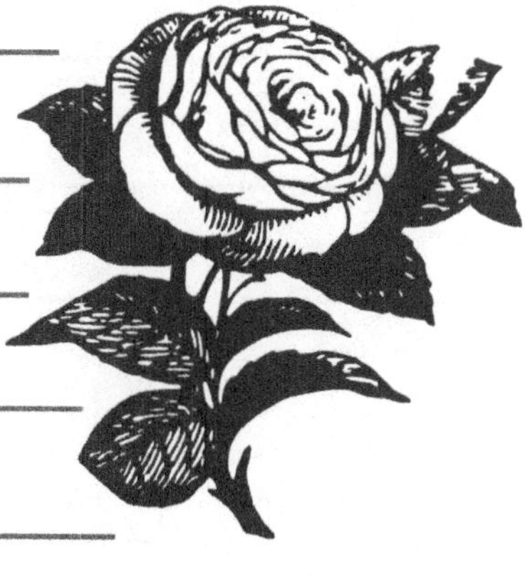

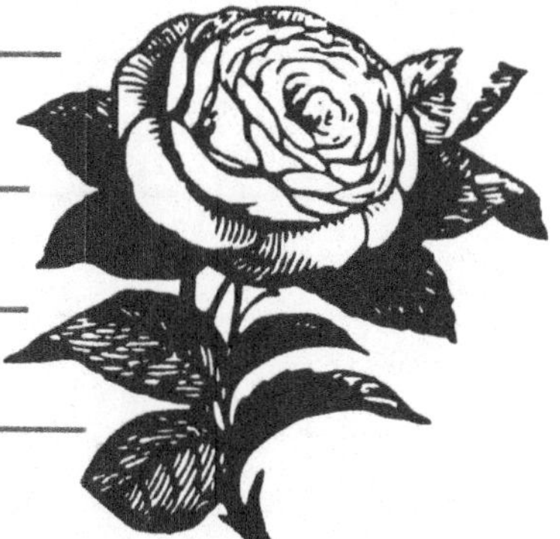

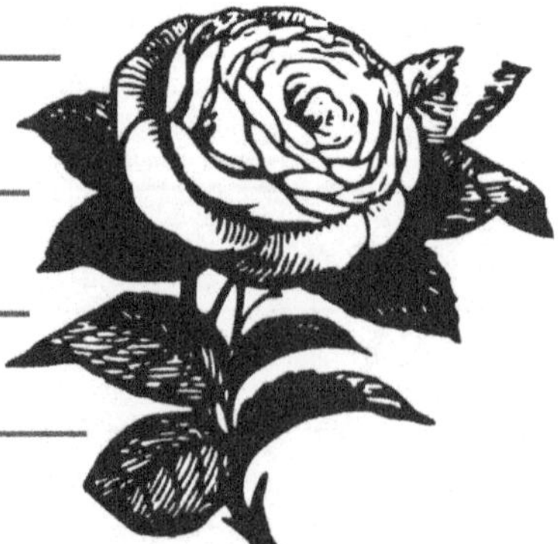

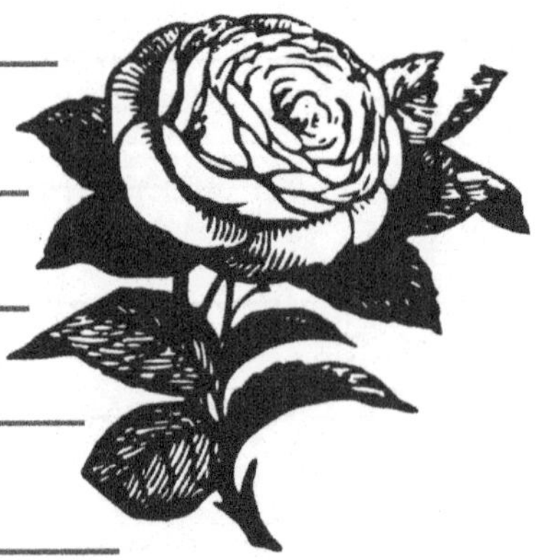

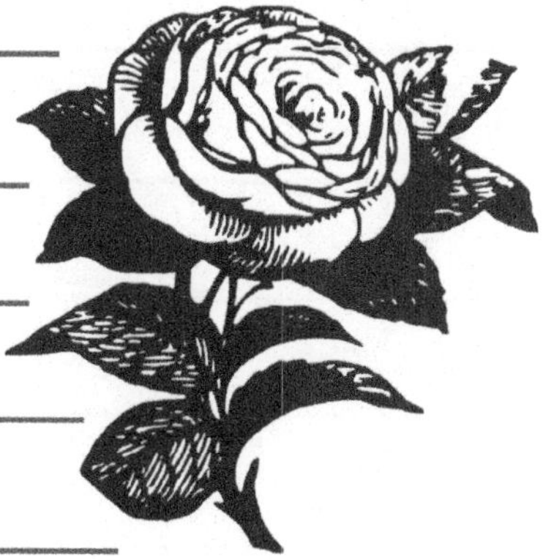

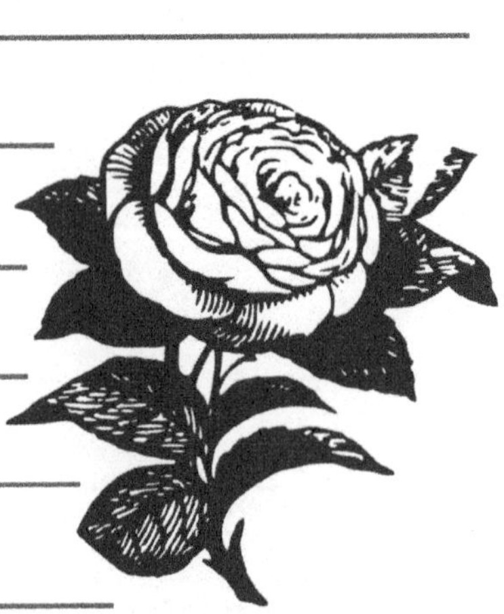

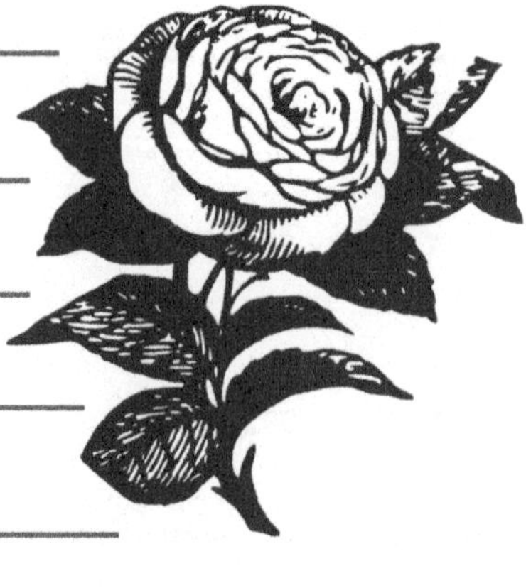

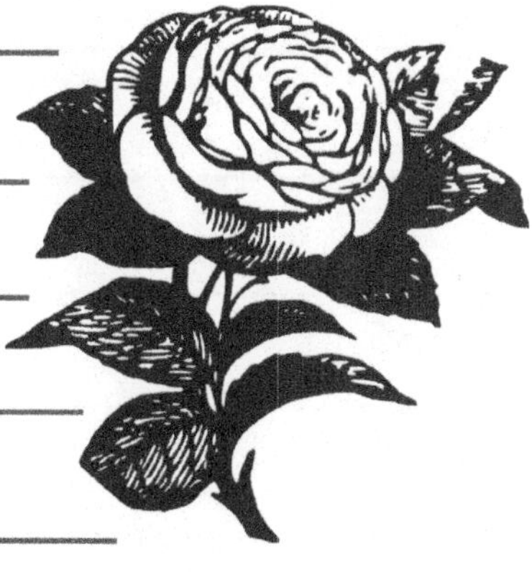

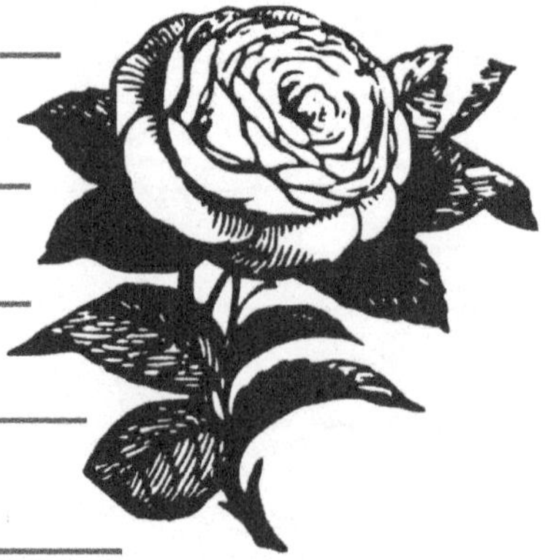

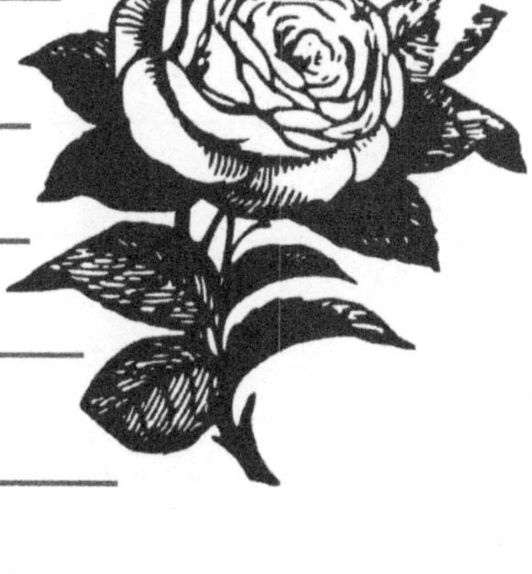

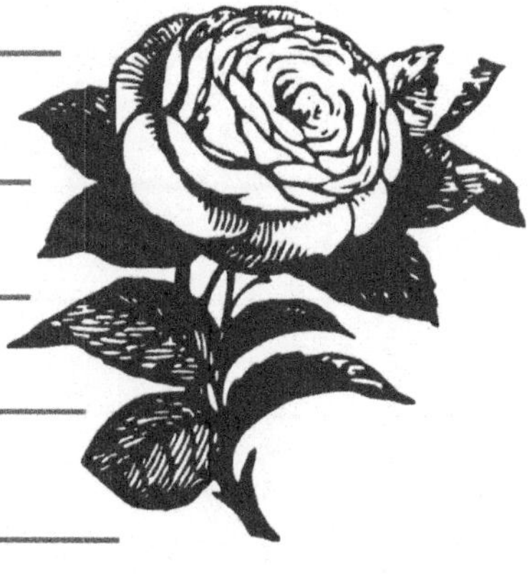

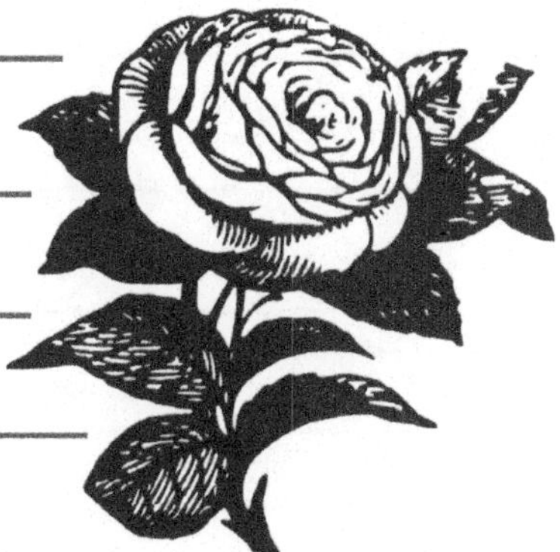

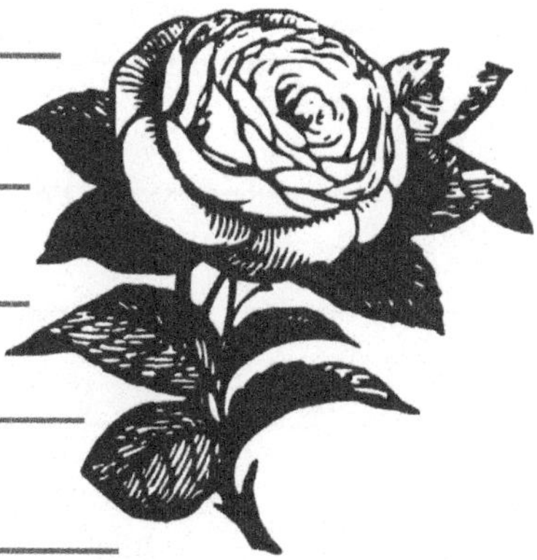

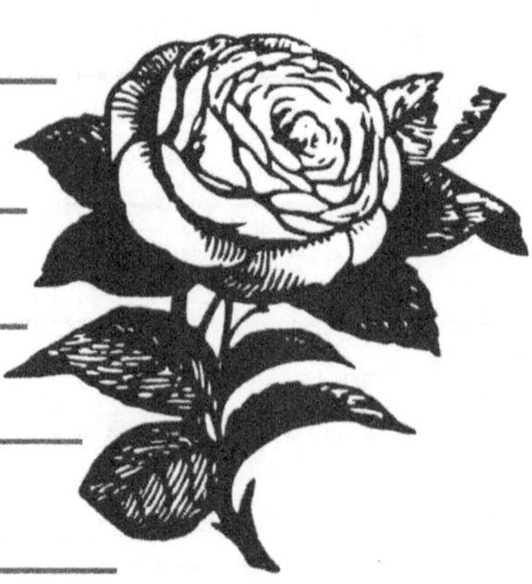

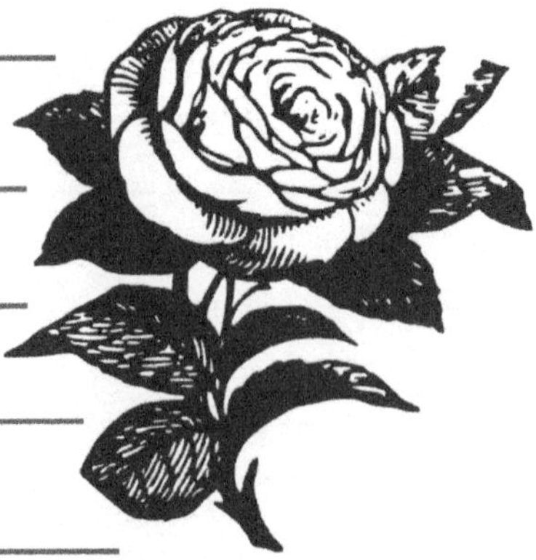

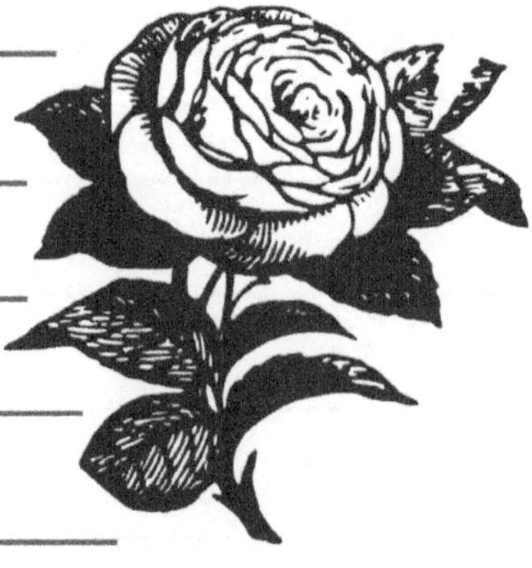

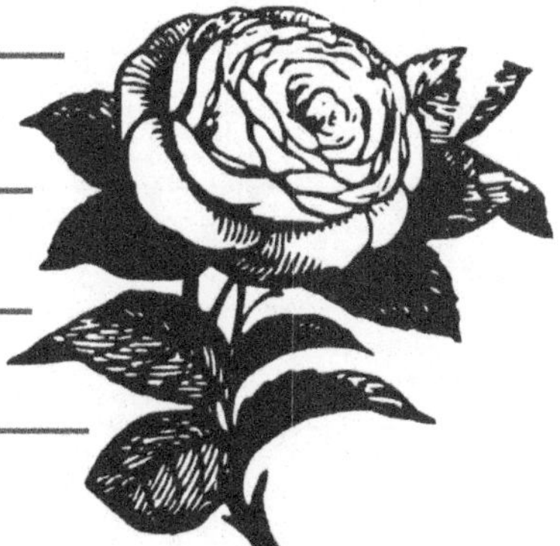

Made in the USA
Monee, IL
25 March 2022

93505050R00073